JOSUHA TREE

Hike. Contemplate what makes you happy and what makes you happier still. Follow a trail or blaze a new one. **Hike**. Think about what you can do to expand your life and someone else's. **Hike**. Slow down. Gear up. **Hike**. Connect with friends. Re-connect with nature.

Hike. Shed stress. Feel blessed. **Hike** to remember. **Hike** to forget. **Hike** for recovery. **Hike** for discovery. **Hike**. Enjoy the beauty of providence. **Hike**. Share the way, The Hiker's Way, on the long and winding trail we call life.

HIKE
JOSHUA TREE

BY
JOHN MCKINNEY

TheTrailmaster.com

HIKE Joshua Tree By John McKinney

ISBN: 978-0934161-91-6
Book Design by Lisa DeSpain
Cartography by Brandi Webber
HIKE Series Editor: Cheri Rae

Published by Olympus Press and The Trailmaster, Inc.
(Visit our site TheTrailmaster.com for a complete listing of all Trailmaster publications, products, and services.)

Although The Trailmaster, Inc. and the author have made every attempt to ensure that information in this book is accurate, they are not responsible for any loss, damage, injury, or inconvenience that may occur to you while using this information. You are responsible for your own safety; the fact that an activity or trail is described in this book does not mean it will be safe for you. Trail conditions can change from day to day; always check local conditions and know your limitations.

Contents

Lost Horse Valley

Queen Valley

Pinto Basin & Cottonwood Spring

Sunset over Ryan Mountain, one of the splendid places to hike in Joshua Tree National Park.

EVERY TRAIL TELLS A STORY.

INTRODUCTION

Those Joshua trees sure are photogenic: framed by big boulders, a grove of them in sunset colors, an isolated specimen in silhouette.

The Joshua tree's distribution defines the very boundaries of the Mojave Desert. Here in its namesake national park, it reaches the southernmost limit of its range.

For many visitors, including hikers, the Joshua trees are the essence, even the whole of their park experience. But there's more, much more to experience.

Joshua Tree National Park is much more than a tableau of twisted yucca. The park beckons hikers with pathways leading to a diversity of desert environments, including sand dunes, native palm oases, cactus gardens and jumbles of jumbo granite.

Joshua Tree is a great place to take a hike. And there's a lot of park to hike!

JT is a large national park, slightly larger than Yosemite in fact, with compelling sights-to-see scattered over nearly 800,000 acres. With elevations that range from 900 feet to more than 5,000 feet, the park has a great deal of biodiversity as well.

With limited time, it's best to choose a strategy to explore Joshua Tree. One approach is to focus on one area per visit: Cottonwood Springs, Black Rock Canyon or the Wonderland of Rocks for example. Another way to go is to choose one route of travel—say from the West Entrance or North Entrance—and stop for hikes along major park roads.

Another strategy to employ is to take a lot of short hikes. The park has a dozen interpreted nature trails ranging from 0.25 mile to 1 mile in length. They travel over gentle terrain and offer an ideal introduction to the wonders of the desert.

In combination with stops at the park visitor centers, the park's nature trails deliver an excellent overview of the park. Taking several short hikes in a day is a good way to go for the first-time visitor as well as for those new to desert hiking, and who may be unfamiliar with its rigors and requirements.

In Joshua Tree, hikers have the opportunity to experience two deserts: the Mojave and the Colorado. The Mojave Desert in the western part of the park includes Joshua tree forests and some intriguing geology—particularly the dramatic hills of bare rock, usually broken up into loose boulders. Along with the Joshua trees that dominate the open spaces, the park

Don't miss hiking JT's many nature trails, like the one to Arch Rock.

also holds enclaves of pinyon pine, California juniper and the desert scrub oak.

Below 3,000 feet, the eastern part of the park reflects the Colorado Desert—with habitats of creosote bush, ocotillo, yucca and cholla cactus. This lower and drier desert features cactus gardens and dunes, plus palm oases, where water occurs naturally year-around and the native California fan palm thrives.

Paths to palm oases are one of the park's special attractions. Oasis Visitor Center is located alongside the Oasis of Mara, also known as Twenty-nine Palms. For many hundreds of years Native Americans lived at "the place of little springs and much grass."

Cottonwood Spring, near the south end of the park is a little palm and cottonwood-shaded oasis that

attracts desert birds and bird-watchers. The trail to
Fortynine Palms Oasis winds up and over a hot rocky
crest to the dripping springs, pools, and the blessed
shade of palms and cottonwoods. Lost Palms Oasis
Trail visits the park's most populous palm grove.

No visit to JT would be complete without a short
hike into the Wonderland of Rocks, twelve square
miles of massive jumbled granite. This curious maze
of stone hides groves of Joshua trees, trackless washes
and several small pools of water.

Hikers often cross paths with rock-climbers and
spot them practicing their craft on formations high
above the desert floor. From Hidden Valley to the
Wonderland of Rocks, the park has emerged as one of
the world's premiere rock-climbing destinations. The
park offers relatively easy access to about 3,000 climb-
ing routes, ranging from the easiest of bouldering to
some of the sport's most difficult technical climbs.

The Jumbo Rocks area is Joshua Tree National
Park to the max: a vast array of rock formations, a
Joshua tree forest, the yucca-dotted desert open and
wide. Check out Skull Rock (one of the many rocks
in the area that appear to resemble humans, dino-
saurs, monsters, cathedrals and castles) via a nature
trail that provides an introduction to the park's flora,
wildlife and geology.

In Queen Valley, just west of Jumbo Rocks, is the
signed beginning of Geology Tour Road, a rough

dirt road (four-wheel drive recommended) extending 18 miles into the heart of the park. Motorists get close-up looks at the considerable erosive forces that shaped this land, forming the flattest of desert playas, or dry lakebeds, as well as massive heaps of boulders that tower over the valley floor. Good hikes begin off Geology Tour Road, which delivers a Joshua tree woodland, an historic spring, abandoned mines and some fascinating native petroglyphs.

One of my favorite footpaths is Black Rock Canyon Trail, which follows a classic desert wash, then ascends to the crest of the Little San Bernardino Mountains at Warren Peak. Desert and mountain views from the peak are stunning.

Must-do classic hikes include the short but steep ascent through a lunar landscape of rocks and Joshua trees to the top of 5,470-foot Ryan Mountain. Reward for the climb is one of the park's best views. Lost Horse Mine Trail visits one of the area's most successful gold mines, and offers a close-up look back into a colorful era, and some fine views into the heart of the park.

Hike smart, reconnect with nature and have a wonderful time on the trail.

Hike on.

—John McKinney

*From Keys View, look out at a meeting of
high and low deserts.*

EVERY TRAIL TELLS A STORY.

JOSHUA TREE NATIONAL PARK

Geography

Extending along the border of two large Southern California counties (Riverside and San Bernardino), the park is named for the Joshua tree, signature tree of the Mojave Desert. At 790,636 acres, Joshua Tree National Park is slightly larger than the state of Rhode Island. More than half (429,690 acres) of the park is designated wilderness area.

The park area is sometimes known as the "connecting" desert because of its location between the Mojave and Colorado deserts, and because it shares characteristics of each. The Mojave, a desert of mountains, is (relatively) cooler-wetter-higher and forms the northern and western parts of the park. Southern and eastern sections of the park are part of the hotter-drier-lower Colorado Desert.

Two paved roads explore the heart of the park. The first loops through the high northwest section, visiting Queen and Lost Horse Valleys, as well as the awesome boulder piles at Jumbo Rocks and Wonderland of Rocks. The second angles northwest-southeast across the park, and crosses both the Mojave Desert Joshua tree woodland and cactus gardens of the Colorado Desert.

Natural History

The Colorado Desert portion of the park is characterized by a wide variety of desert flora, including ironwood, smoke tree and native California fan palms. Cacti, especially cholla and ocotillo, thrive in the more southerly Colorado Desert (a part of the larger Sonoran Desert).

Higher and (slightly) cooler Mojave Desert environs of the park feature Joshua trees as well as the famed granite monoliths.

Low and behold: The desert tortoise is a slow-moving photo subject for sure.

Along with its two distinct desert environments, the park boasts a third ecosystem: At higher elevations (above 4,000 feet) the Little San Bernardino Mountains host communities of pinyon pine and California juniper.

JT is located on the Pacific Flyway and more than 250 species of migratory and resident birds have been sighted in the park, including the cactus wren, roadrunner and Gambel's quail. Best bird-watching spots include Queen Valley and Lost Horse Valley, plus places with water such as Barker Dam and the various palm oases. Visitors frequently spot ground squirrels, lizards and jackrabbits and more occasionally coyotes, bighorn sheep or one of the park's six (!) species of rattlesnakes.

In close-up, the greater roadrunner clearly looks like it belongs to the cuckoo family.

Native Peoples

Native peoples—the Serrano, Chemehuevi and Cahuilla tribes—lived in what is now Joshua Tree National Park long before the arrival of Europeans in 1769. The Chemehuevi, for example, are believed to have migrated into the area more than 400 years ago, and their territories included Pinto Basin and the Coxcomb Mountains. Both the Serrano and Cahuilla lived at the Oasis of Mara.

Despite its outwardly barren and hostile appearance, the desert land provided an abundance of resources. Oases and springs supplied water, rocks and canyons shade and shelter.

Mesquite beans, yucca root, acorns, pinyon nuts were among the dependable food sources. Native

Cahuilla woman

Native American art, property of Joshua Tree National Park

The Cahuilla lived in small villages near water sources in what is now the western and southern portions of JTNP.

peoples hunted deer, rabbits, birds and bighorn sheep. Desert plants were made into bows and arrows, baskets and medicines.

More than 120 plant species have been identified as having been used as food, medicine or as raw materials for making a range of objects from rope to mats to hats. A hostile land? Not for native peoples who were connected with their land and made use of what nature provided.

Rock art reminds us of the spirits of the indigenous people and their intimate connection to the land.

Conservation History

First impressions of the land that would become Joshua Tree National Park were not encouraging. A scout for the U.S. Railroad Survey of 1853 reported: "Nothing is known of this country. I am inclined to the belief that it is barren, mountainous desert composed of a system of basins and mountain ranges. It would be exceedingly difficult country to explore on account of the absence of water and there is not rainy season of any consequence." Nineteenth century cattle ranchers grazed cows in what was once a wetter environment. Miners really put the Joshua Tree area on the map in their far-flung efforts to find gold.

During the 1920s, a worldwide fascination with the desert developed, and cactus gardens were very much in vogue. Entrepreneurs hauled truckloads of desert plants into Los Angeles for quick sale or export.

Thank you Minerva Hoyt, mover and shaker behind the creation of JTNP.

The Mojave was in danger of being picked clean of cacti, yucca and ocotillo. Wealthy socialite Minerva Hoyt organized the International Desert Conservation League to halt this destructive practice. Almost single-handedly, she successfully lobbied for the establishment of Joshua Tree National Monument in 1936.

In 1994, under provisions of the federal California Desert Protection Act, Joshua Tree was "upgraded" from national monument to national park status and expanded by about a quarter-million acres. The park has had to face more than its share of environmental threats in recent years: a mammoth landfill operation on its eastern boundary, sprawling cities on its northern boundary, a proposed city of 10,000 people and several golf courses at its southern boundary, and military flights that crisscross its skies.

In 2012, a 5,405-foot mountain located close to park high point Quail Mountain was named Mount Minerva Hoyt in honor of her tireless desert conservation efforts.

All About the Joshua Tree

The Joshua tree is said to have been given its name by early Mormon settlers traveling the West. The tree's upraised limbs and bearded appearance reminded them of the prophet Joshua leading them to the promised land. Historians, Biblical and not, have been known to quibble about how the name originated and point out that the appearance of the Joshua tree more closely follows a story about Moses. The Moses tree? Seriously?!

Other observers were not so Old Testament and not so kind. Explorer John C. Frémont called it "the most repulsive tree in the vegetable kingdom." Some referred to it as *Izote de desierto*, "Desert dagger" in Spanish.

Nature writer Charles Francis Saunders opined: "The trees themselves were as grotesque as the creations of a bad dream; the shaggy trunks and limbs were twisted and seemed writhing as though in pain, and dagger-pointed leaves were clenched in bristling fists of inhospitality."

Even the author of *California Desert Trails*, Joseph Smeaton Chase, who almost never met a tree he didn't like, wrote: "It is a weird, menacing object, more like some conception of Poe's or Doré's than any work of wholesome Mother Nature. One can scarcely find a term of ugliness that is not apt for this plant."

Despite its harsh appearance, the Joshua tree belongs to the lily family. Like lilies and other flowers, it must be pollinated in order to reproduce. Depending on rainfall, Joshua trees flower from February to late April. When in bloom, the yellow, lily-like flowers are pollinated by the yucca moth, sprinkling pollen as it lays eggs inside of them. Moth larvae eat the seeds, but enough seeds are spared to reproduce.

The Joshua tree provides shelter for a number of small desert animals, particularly rodents, such as the kangaroo rat, desert wood rat, and ground squirrel.

The Joshua Tree, Mojave Desert icon, beloved by desert lovers, faces an uncertain future in the wake of climate change.

Birds, including the pinyon jay, loggerhead shrike and Scott's oriole, make their nests in the gnarled branches.

Their range coincides with the boundaries of the Mojave Desert. In JTNP, Joshua trees are especially numerous on the open terrain of Lost Horse Valley and Queen Valley. The trees grow at the foot of mountain slopes and capture the surface and groundwater draining from higher elevations. Occasionally you'll see a Joshua tree clumsily embrace one of its fellows but, generally, its water requirements keep it distant from other trees.

As desert flora goes, Joshua trees are fast growers. Determining a Joshua's growth rate and age is difficult, though, because the fibrous trunk lacks annual growth rings. Thanks to a deep and far-reaching root

Behold the Joshua Tree in bloom. A member in good standing of the lily family.

system the Joshua tree can survive the challenges of the Mojave and live for hundreds of years; some trees are believed to be a thousand years old.

Nineteenth century ranchers and miners chopped up the Joshua trees and limbs for fencing and to burn fuel in steam-powered ore-processing machines. In the 1920s and 30s, conservationists began to see the Joshua tree region in a new light. Minerva Hamilton Hoyt, appalled at the widespread destruction of so many of the native desert plants and Joshua trees that she found so beautiful, led the effort to create Joshua Tree National Monument, forerunner of the national park.

Climate change, manifested by increased temperatures and prolonged drought, is threatening the very survival of the species. The disastrous Dome Fire destroyed one of the planet's finest Joshua Tree forests in the Cima Dome area of JT's sister park, Mojave National Preserve, in August 2020. Ecological researchers suggest the Joshua's range will be reduced by as much as 90 percent by the end of the 21st century and the grim possibility the trees could vanish from Joshua Tree National Park. Joshua Tree-less National Park?!

While we rightly should be alarmed and take action on behalf of the Joshua tree, perhaps we can also be inspired by this icon of the Mojave Desert. As author Jeannette Walls puts it: "It's the Joshua tree's struggle that gives it its beauty."

Administration

For visitor information about Joshua Tree National Park call 760-367-5500 or visit nps.gov/jotr. Joshua Tree Visitor Center, operated in partnership with the Joshua Tree National Park Association, is located one block south of Hwy 62 (Twentynine Palms Highway) at 6554 Park Boulevard in the town of Joshua Tree. Open all year, 8 a.m. to 5 p.m. daily. Check for schedules of guided hikes and interpretive programs.

More visitor information is available at Oasis Visitor Center at the Twentynine Palms entrance, Cottonwood at the south entrance, and Black Rock Canyon, located at the campground southeast of Yucca Valley.

Along with his colleagues, this ranger at Cottonwood Spring has a lot of park to patrol. JTNP is larger than the state of Rhode Island.

Joshua Tree National Park Association is the nonprofit support group for the park. (760-367-5525, or visit JoshuaTree.org)

No restaurants, lodging, gas stations or stores are found within Joshua Tree National Park. In fact, water is available only from four park locations: Cottonwood Springs, Blackrock Canyon Campground, Indian Cove Ranger Station and Oasis Visitor Center.

One short hike, two vast deserts.
Get a great view of the transition between the
Mojave and Colorado deserts from High View Trail.

EVERY TRAIL TELLS A STORY.

I

BLACK ROCK CANYON

HIKE ON.

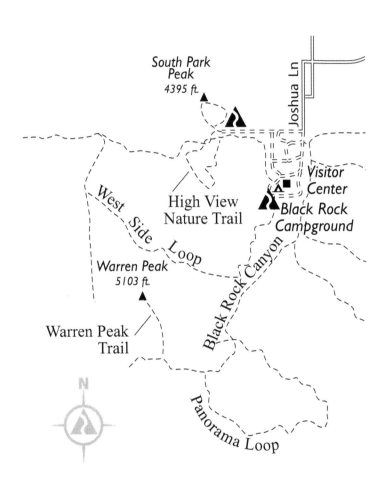

South Park
Peak
4395 ft.

Joshua Ln

Visitor
Center

Black Rock
Campground

High View
Nature Trail

West Side Loop

Warren Peak
5103 ft.

Black Rock Canyon

Warren Peak
Trail

N

Panorama Loop

HIGH VIEW

HIGH VIEW NATURE TRAIL

1.3 mile-loop with 300-foot elevation gain

If one word could sum up view from High View, it might be "transitions." That is, transitions between the Mojave and Colorado deserts and between fast-growing desert cities and JTNP.

An interpretive brochure (available at the visitor center) explains the region's ecology.

DIRECTIONS: From Black Rock Road at the campground entrance, turn right (west) and go 0.8 miles to the end of the dirt road.

THE HIKE: Meander past tall yuccas and ascend up and around pinyon pine-dotted slopes. Benches offer the hiker rest and places from which to regard the surrounding desert. The trail passes the Joshua tree and its close cousin the nolina.

Reach the summit at the 0.5-mile mark and enjoy clear-day views.

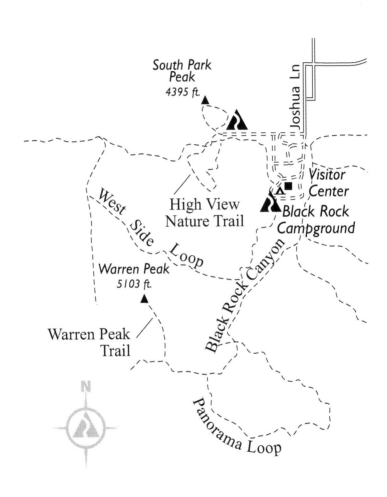

South Park
Peak
4395 ft.

Joshua Ln

Visitor
Center

West Side Loop

High View
Nature Trail

Black Rock
Campground

Black Rock Canyon

Warren Peak
5103 ft.

Warren Peak
Trail

N

Panorama Loop

BLACK ROCK CANYON

BLACK ROCK CANYON TRAIL

From Black Rock Campground to Warren Peak is 5.5 miles round trip with 1,000-foot elevation gain

A hike through Black Rock Canyon has just about everything a desert hike should have: plenty of cactus, pinyon pine-dotted peaks, a sandy wash, dramatic rock formations, a hidden spring, grand vistas. Tucked away in the northwest corner of the park, the area also hosts forests of the shaggy Joshuas.

More than 200 species of birds, including speedy roadrunners, have been observed in and around Black Rock Canyon. Hikers frequently spot mule deer and rabbits—desert cottontails and black-tailed jackrabbits.

Black Rock Canyon rarely makes the "must see" list of JT's natural attractions, even though it is one of the easiest places to reach. The canyon is close to Yucca Valley's commercial strip and residential neighborhoods and yet matches the allure of much more remote regions of the national park.

Black Rock Canyon Trail follows a classic desert wash, and then ascends to Warren Peak at the wild west end of the Little San Bernardino Mountains. Desert and mountain views from the peak are stunning.

DIRECTIONS: From Highway 62 in Yucca Valley, turn south on Joshua Lane and drive 4.6 miles to a T-intersection. Turn right then bend left on Black Rock Canyon Road, which leads a mile to Black Rock Campground. Park near the visitor center and walk up to the trailhead by campsite #30.

THE HIKE: From the upper end of the campground, the trail leads 0.2 mile to a water tank, goes left a very short distance on a park service road, then immediately angles right, continuing east.

About 0.6 mile from the trailhead, the path drops into the dry, sandy creekbed of Black Rock Canyon. Bear right and head up the wide canyon mouth, passing Joshua trees, desert willow and cholla. Signs reading "WP" for Warren Peak keep the hiker on track.

Wash-walking leads to the remains of some so-called "tanks," or rock basins built by early ranchers to hold water for cattle. Farther up the wash is Black Rock Spring, sometimes dry, sometimes a trickle. Beyond the spring, the canyon narrows. Wend your way around beavertail cactus, pinyon pine and juniper.

Stay right at a junction (with the Panorama Loop Trail heading left), and a second right in 0.4 mile where the loop trail rejoins the trail to Warren Peak. Continue 0.3 mile to a Y junction; the spur trail to the left leads to Warren View. Stay right and climb to a dramatic ridge crest of the Little San Bernardino Mountains, then angle right (west) along the crest. The rough trail ascends steeply 0.4 mile (with a 400-foot gain) past contorted wind-blown juniper and pinyon pine to the top of Warren Peak.

What a grand clear-day view! Look north to the Mojave Desert, west to the San Bernardino Mountains; to the southwest behold mighty Mt. San Jacinto, Palm Springs and the Coachella Valley.

The Panorama Loop is an awesome add-on to the Warren Peak hike.

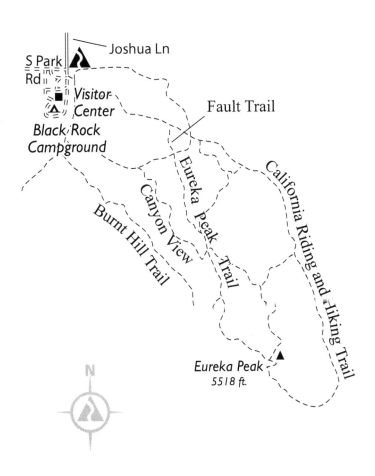

Joshua Ln

S Park Rd

Visitor Center

Black Rock Campground

Fault Trail

Eureka Peak Trail

Canyon View

Burnt Hill Trail

California Riding and Hiking Trail

Eureka Peak
5518 ft.

N

EUREKA PEAK

CALIFORNIA RIDING & HIKING, FAULT TRAIL, EUREKA PEAK, BURNT HILL TRAILS

From Black Rock Canyon Campground to Eureka Peak is 10 miles round trip with 1,500-foot elevation gain

Clear-day panoramic views from 5,518-foot Eureka Peak are among the best in the national park. During winter and spring, snow-capped Mt. San Jacinto towers over the Coachella Valley. Mt. San Gorgonio, highest peak in SoCal, and other 10,000-foot summits in the San Gorgonio Wilderness, are a majestic sight. And yes, that's Palm Springs visible to the southwest.

True, motorists can drive remote dirt roads nearly to the top of Eureka Peak, but not that many do. This hike with its combination of washes, ridges and ravines, as well as some trail-less sections definitely appeals to the hiker's sense of adventure—more of a wilderness experience than you might expect from an

outing so close to a park entrance and nearby civilization. From Black Rock Campground, California
Riding and Hiking Trail and Eureka Peak Trail ascend the hills fringing the Yucca Valley and leads to a
series of washes and narrow canyons that you follow
to the summit of Eureka Peak, fourth highest in the
national park. Signposts help in negotiating the trail-
less stretches of the route. Burnt Hill Trail is a good
choice for a return route.

DIRECTIONS: From Highway 62 in Yucca
Valley, turn south on Joshua Lane and drive 4.6 miles
to a T-intersection. Turn right on San Marino Drive,
which bends left to become Black Rock Canyon Road
and leads a mile to Black Rock Campground. The trail
begins at the Black Canyon information board located
just outside the entry to the campground.

THE HIKE: From the information board, hike
southwest 0.2 mile to a junction. Note Black Rock
Canyon heading south and turn left (east) on the
CR&HT. Pass through pretty country dotted with
Joshua trees, pinyon pine and juniper, get a view of
Yucca Valley. At 1.3 miles meet Fault Trail and go
right, which ascend for 0.25 mile then descends into
a wash. About 1.7 miles out, turn right on Eureka
Peak Trail.

Begin two miles-plus of wash walking, following
Eureka Peak Trail on a southeast climb amidst yuccas and pinyon pine. Pass a left fork with Cliff Trail,

a right fork with Canyon View Trail, and a junction with Burnt Hill Trail (an optional return route).

Continue your ascent. The wash narrows at the 4-mile mark, you climb to a saddle, descend briefly, and pass a junction with Bigfoot Trail. Cresting a ridge, continue to angle south-southeast around to the south side of Eureka Peak. Lastly, join the short summit trail (and those motorists taking the easy way to the top!) ascending from the parking area.

Retrace your steps all the way back. Or descend to meet Burnt Hill Trail, and join this path which ascends 0.4 mile to a saddle. Then make a lengthy descent along slopes populated with Joshua trees and pinyon pine to reach Black CanyonTrail; follow this trail 0.8 mile back to the trailhead.

Far-out views to the west from Eureka Peak.

Turkey vultures circling—an unusual sight in the skies above the Oasis of Mara.

EVERY TRAIL TELLS A STORY.

II

West Entrance & Oasis Visitor Center

HIKE ON.

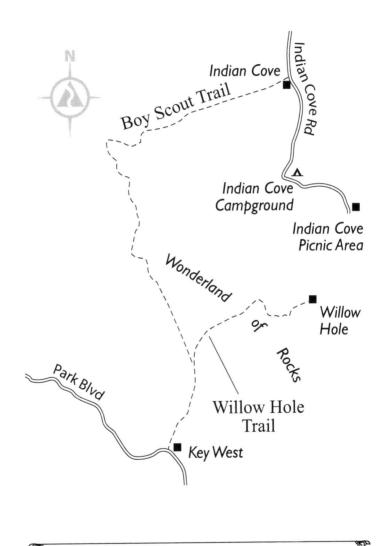

Indian Cove

Boy Scout Trail

Indian Cove Rd

Indian Cove
Campground

Indian Cove
Picnic Area

Wonderland

of

Rocks

Willow
Hole

Park Blvd

Willow Hole
Trail

Key West

WONDERLAND AND WILLOW HOLE

BOY SCOUT TRAIL

Park Boulevard to Indian Cove Road is 7.8 miles one way with 1,300-foot elevation loss; to Willow Hole is 7.2 miles round trip

One of the park's outstanding footpaths, Boy Scout Trail tours a quintessential Joshua Tree National Park landscape: a vast array of rock formations, a Joshua tree forest, the yucca-dotted desert open and wide. It skirts the wild western edge of the Wonderland of Rocks, and travels along narrow, sandy canyons dotted with pinyon pine and juniper.

And, if the allure of this uncommon landscape is not sufficient motivation to take this hike, it boasts one more attraction: it's a nearly all-downhill hike.

Boy Scout Trail is commonly enjoyed as a one-way trek aided by a car shuttle. Usually hikers prefer the downhill walk from Keys View trailhead to the Indian Cove trailhead. A terrific add-on is the 4-mile round trip to Willow Hole, a seasonal spring surrounded by willows.

DIRECTIONS: From Highway 62 in the town of Joshua Tree, turn south on Park Boulevard and drive 5 miles to the west entrance of Joshua Tree National Park. Continue another 7 miles to Keys View Backcountry Board and the trailhead, located on the left (north) side of the road. Car shuttle: From Highway 62, 10 miles east of the town of Joshua Tree and the Park Boulevard turnoff, turn south on Indian Cove Road and proceed 1.5 miles to the Indian Cove trailhead on the right (west) side of the road.

THE HIKE: Boy Scout Trail climbs gently through a Joshua tree forest. As it travels along the west side of the Wonderland of Rocks, views open up to the southwest of the sometimes snowcapped San Bernardino Mountains.

At a signed junction 1.25 miles from the trailhead, the path forks. The left fork is the continuation of Boy Scout Trail; the right branch leads to Willow Hole. (Willow Hole-bound hikers will join the sandy trail on a mellow 1.2-mile descent past granite towers to a wash, then follow the wash 0.8 mile to willow lined seasonal pools tucked in a cliff-encircled rock bowl.)

Boy Scout Trail traverses a fairly flat, Joshua tree- and yucca-dotted plateau. About 3 miles from the trailhead, the path meanders amidst pinyon pine, oak and juniper and drops into a rocky canyon, where park service markers help you stay on the trail; at 3.5 miles, the trail follows a wash and at 4 miles, this hike's halfway point, pass a cement water tank.

After another 0.25 mile of wash-walking, concentrate on sticking with the trail, which exits the wash and bends sharply to the west. The now rocky trail dips and rises, then switchbacks down to another wash at the 5-mile mark. After a mile of wash-walking, the path crosses over to a second, wider wash, and follows the latter for 0.5 mile.

The trail climbs out of the wash and crosses a broad alluvial fan spiked with cholla and yucca. A final 1.5 miles of walking across the fan leads to the Indian Cove trailhead.

"Be prepared," as the Boy Scouts say, to hike one of JT's most outstanding trails.

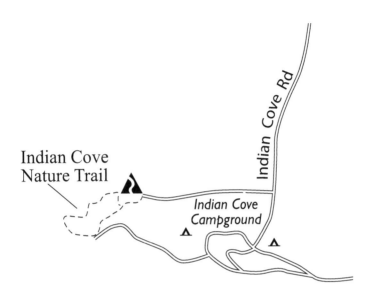

Indian Cove
Nature Trail

Indian Cove Rd

Indian Cove
Campground

N

Rattlesnake Canyon

Indian Cove

Indian Cove Nature Trail

0.6 mile round trip

Long before park visitors pulled trailers and pitched tents in the cove, native peoples stopped here on winter migrations. Indian Cove Nature Trail interprets desert flora and offers history of the earliest human inhabitants.

DIRECTIONS: From Highway 62, some 7 miles west of Twentynine Palms and 10 miles east of Joshua Tree (the town), turn south on Indian Cove Road and drive 3 miles south to Indian Cove Campground. Follow the signs to the parking area for the signed nature trail.

THE HIKE: The path begins in the shadow of boulders, the northern fringe of the Wonderland of Rocks. Rock overhangs and caves offered shelter to the native Serrano. Descend into a wash, loop past the curious paperbag bush and assorted cacti then ascend out of the wash.

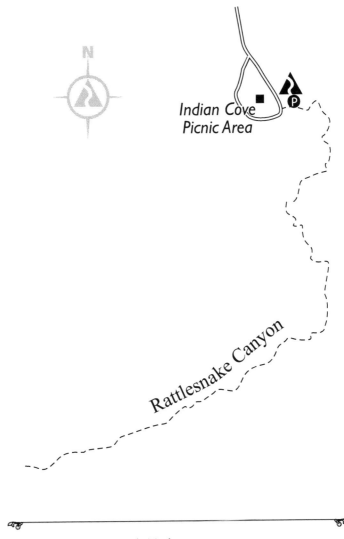

Indian Cove
Picnic Area

Rattlesnake Canyon

RATTLESNAKE CANYON

RATTLESNAKE CANYON TRAIL

1 to 3 miles round trip

Considering this part of JT is so dry, it's surprising to discover a (seasonal) little creek tumbling over the boulder-strewn Rattlesnake Canyon. A half-mile from the mouth of the canyon is a small waterfall, where the creek tumbles over the polished rocks. Tiny cascades and lovely pools complete the attractive scene.

DIRECTIONS: From Yucca Valley, drive east on Highway 62 for 14 miles to Indian Cove Road. Turn south (right), proceed a mile to the ranger station, then 3.3 more miles to the picnic area and unsigned trail at road's end.

THE HIKE: Walk east into the creekbed of Rattlesnake Canyon. Head south (up-canyon) dodging creosote bush and yucca and working your way around boulders to the base of the falls.

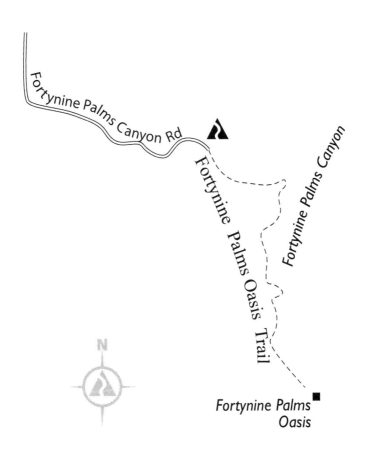

Fortynine Palms Canyon Rd

Fortynine Palms Oasis Trail

Fortynine Palms Canyon

N

Fortynine Palms
Oasis

FORTY-NINE PALMS

FORTY-NINE PALMS TRAIL

To Forty-nine Palms Oasis is 3 miles round trip with 350-foot elevation gain

Forty-nine Palms Oasis has retained a wonderful air of remoteness. An old trail climbs a steep ridge and offers the hiker expansive views of the Sheephole and Bullion mountain ranges.

On the exposed ridge, barrel cacti, creosote, yucca, and brittlebush brave the heat. As the trail winds up and over a rocky crest, the restful green of the oasis comes into view.

At the oasis, nature's personality abruptly changes and the dry, sun-baked ridges give way to dripping springs, pools, and the blessed shade of palms and cottonwoods.

Unlike those oases strung out for miles along a stream, Forty-nine Palms Oasis is a close-knit palm family centered on a generous supply of surface water. Seeps and springs fill numerous basins set among the rocks at different levels. Mesquite and willow thrive alongside the palms. Singing house finches and croaking frogs provide a musical interlude.

Perched on a steep canyon wall, Forty-nine Palms Oasis overlooks the town of Twentynine Palms, but its untouched beauty makes it seem a lot farther removed from civilization.

DIRECTIONS: From Highway 62 about 5.5 miles west of Twentynine Palms and 11 miles east of the town of Joshua Tree, turn south on Fortynine Palms Canyon Road and follow it 2 miles to its end at a National Park Service parking area and the trailhead.

THE HIKE: The trail rises through a Spartan rockscape dotted with cacti and jojoba. After a brisk climb, catch your breath atop a ridgetop and enjoy the view of Twentynine Palms and the surrounding desert.

Colorful patches of lichen adhere to the rocks. Lichen, which conducts the business of life as a limited partnership of algae and fungi, is very sensitive to air pollution; the health of this tiny plant is considered by some botanists to be related to air quality. Contemplate the abstract impressionist patterns of the lichen, inhale great draughts of fresh air, then follow the trail as it descends from the ridgetop.

The trail leads down slopes dotted with barrel cactus and mesquite. Soon the oasis comes into view. Lucky hikers may get a fleeting glimpse of bighorn sheep drinking from oasis pools or gamboling over nearby steep slopes.

As the path leads to the palms, notice many fire-blackened tree trunks. The grove has burned several times before—and after—its inclusion in the national park.

Forty-nine Palms Oasis celebrates life. Native California fan palm cluster near handsome boulder-lined pools. Fuzzy cattails, ferns and grasses sway in the breeze. An oasis like this one gives the hiker a chance to view the desert in terms that are the exact opposite of its stereotypical dry hostility. If the desert is the land God forgot, then the Creator must have had a sudden afterthought and decided to sprinkle this parched land with oases, reminders of His lush handiwork.

Forty-nine Palms, a true oasis where a close-knit family of palms thrives.

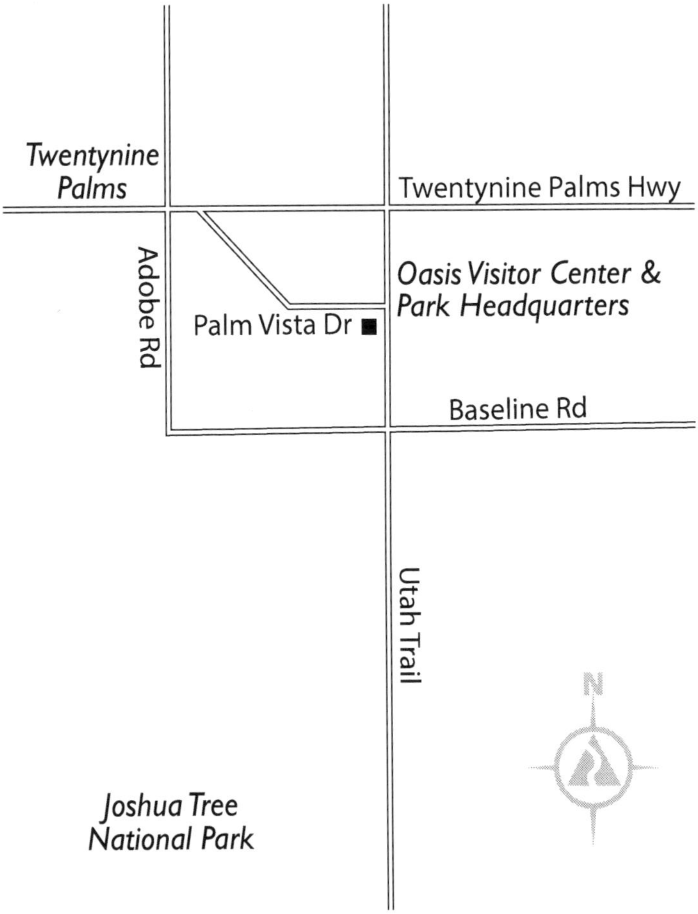

Twentynine Palms
Twentynine Palms Hwy
Adobe Rd
Oasis Visitor Center & Park Headquarters
Palm Vista Dr
Baseline Rd
Utah Trail
N
Joshua Tree National Park

TheTrailmaster.com

OASIS VISITOR CENTER

OASIS OF MARA TRAIL

From Oasis Visitor Center, a 0.5-mile loop

To the native Serrano, *Mara* meant "the place of small springs and much grass." Ranchers, gold seekers, health seekers and generations of desert travelers have stopped at the peaceful oasis.

Check out the interpretive exhibits at Oasis Visitor Center, which has served as park headquarters and as a primary visitor center since 1950.

DIRECTIONS: Oasis Visitor Center (and park headquarters) is located just outside Twentynine Palms on National Park Drive.

Open all year; 8 a.m. to 5 p.m.

THE HIKE: A paved nature trail leads under rustling palms to the famed "Twentynine Palms Oasis," perhaps California's most famous (and certainly the most accessible) palm oasis. Learn how the palms provided the Serrano with food, clothing and shelter.

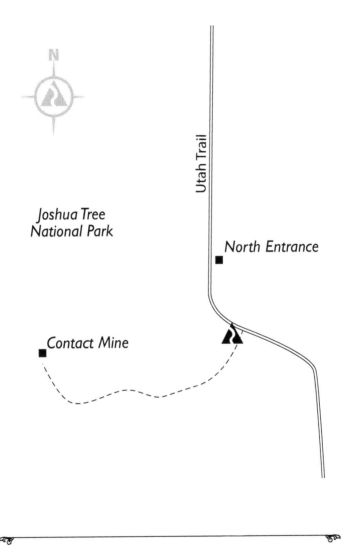

Joshua Tree
National Park

Utah Trail

North Entrance

Contact Mine

TheTrailmaster.com

CONTACT MINE

CONTACT MINE TRAIL

From Park Route 12 to Contact Mine is 3.4 miles round trip with 700-foot elevation gain

Explore an early 1900s' silver and gold mine site on a trail leading into rugged terrain near the park's north entry station. The Contact Mine's considerable remains include several mine shafts, ore car tracks and a cable winch.

The mine's layout, equipment, and the road leading to it all suggest some excellent early 20th century engineering was carefully applied to the endeavor. The access road with its supporting rock foundations and the way it contours over rocky slopes is a particularly good expression of the road-builder's art. Of course, by the standards of the day, the yield from the Contact Mine was good and the enterprise relatively prosperous, so constructing a good access road to the site made good business sense.

Two words of advice about the old road, now a hiking trail. The first stretch of trail is sketchy and you don't actually join the mine road until past the half-mile mark. Also, more than a century of erosion has made this road a rocky one.

DIRECTIONS: From Highway 62 in Twenty-nine Palms, drive 4 miles south on Utah Trail to an entry kiosk on the national park's north boundary. Continue another 0.5 mile south to a pullout, parking and information board on the right (west) side of the road. Last time I hiked this trail, no info was posted about the mine or the hike to it.

THE HIKE: From the information board, follow the very faint road southwest across flat, sandy, cholla-dotted terrain. After 0.1 mile the trail crosses a low dirt dike and soon reaches a second dike that traces a wash. Follow the wash to the right as it curves toward the mountains.

At 0.4 mile, the wash forks and you bear right, heading toward those rocky mountains. Concentrate on the trail but do look up to admire vistas of the Pinto Mountains and the surrounding parkland.

About 0.75 mile of travel from the trailhead brings you to a not-very-obvious junction with another wash. Watch for rock cairns, bear right, climb out of the wash and join the old mining road.

The quite rocky road ascends rapidly for a mile. Along this steep length, the quality of the road construction is particularly evident. Not long after you spot the first mining equipment, the old road delivers you to the ruins of the Contact Mine.

From road's end just below the mine, pick your way across a slope amidst rusted machinery. Angle around to the mine, where you'll find more machinery, rail tracks and covered mine shafts. Be careful around the shafts and mine site debris.

*Imagine a…well, you never know
what you'll see in the Wonderland of Rocks.*

EVERY TRAIL TELLS A STORY.

III

LOST HORSE VALLEY

HIKE ON.

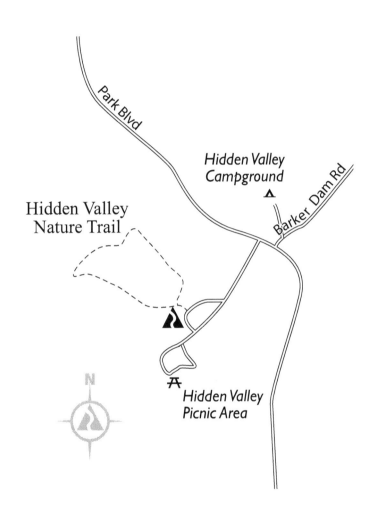

Park Blvd

Hidden Valley
Campground

Barker Dam Rd

Hidden Valley
Nature Trail

N

Hidden Valley
Picnic Area

HIDDEN VALLEY

HIDDEN VALLEY TRAIL

1 mile round trip

With its Joshua trees, rock formations, and an excellent interpretive trail that highlights the rich history of the region, Hidden Valley has long been a favorite of park visitors. The valley's walls are very popular with rock climbers.

DIRECTIONS: From Highway 62 in Joshua Tree, proceed 14 miles south on Park Boulevard to the signed turnoff for Hidden Valley Picnic Area and Nature Trail. Turn right and proceed 0.1 mile to parking and the signed trailhead.

THE HIKE: The path travels between big boulders. Hike past the varied vegetation that keeps company with the Joshuas: turbinella oak, juniper, and pinyon pine, as well as cholla and beavertail cactus.

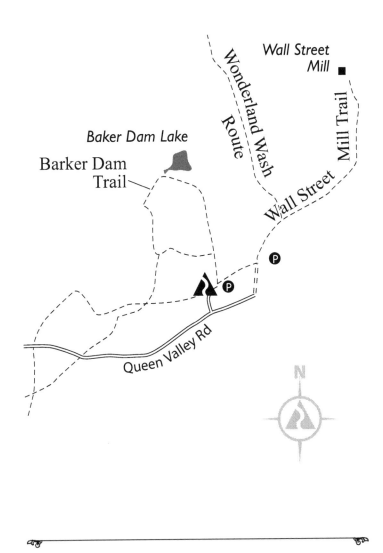

Wall Street
Mill

Wonderland Wash Route

Wall Street

Mill Trail

Baker Dam Lake

Barker Dam
Trail

Queen Valley Rd

N

BARKER DAM AND WONDERLAND OF ROCKS

BARKER DAM NATURE TRAIL

Loop through Wonderland of Rocks to Barker Dam is 1.4 miles

One of the many wonders of Joshua Tree National Park is the Wonderland of Rocks, 12 square miles of massive jumbled granite. This curious maze of stone hides groves of Joshua trees, trackless washes and several small pools of water.

Easiest, and certainly the safest way to explore the Wonderland is to follow the Barker Dam Nature Trail, which interprets the botanical highlights of the area and visits petroglyphs.

This hike's main destination is the small lake created by Barker Dam. A century ago, cowboys took advantage of the water catchment of this natural basin and brought their cattle to this corner of the Wonderland of Rocks. Barker and Shay Cattle Co. constructed the dam, which was later raised to its present height by Bill Keys and his family in the 1950s.

By park service regulation, the area is open only from 8 a.m. to 6 p.m.; this restriction is designed to allow the shy bighorn sheep a chance to reach water without human interference.

DIRECTIONS: From Park Boulevard, 1.5 miles north of the intersection with Keys View Road, turn north on the signed road to Wonderland of Rocks and drive 1.5 miles to the large parking area.

THE HIKE: From the north end of the parking area, join the signed trail that immediately penetrates the Wonderland of Rocks. You'll pass a special kind of oak, the turbinella, which has adjusted to the harsh conditions of desert life.

Interpretive signs point out the unique botany of this desert land. The path squeezes through a narrow rock passageway and leads to the edge of Barker Dam Lake. Bird-watching is excellent here because many migratory species not normally associated with the desert are attracted to the lake. Morning and late afternoon hours are particularly tranquil times to contemplate the ever-changing reflections of the Wonderland of Rocks on the water.

The trail is a bit indistinct near Barker Dam, but resumes again in fine form near a strange-looking circular water trough, a holdover from the area's cattle ranching days. A toilet-like float mechanism controlled the flow of water to the thirsty livestock.

The path turns southerly and soon passes a huge boulder known as Piano Rock. When this land was in private ownership, a piano was hauled atop this rock and played for the amusement of visitors and locals.

Beyond Piano Rock the trail enters a rock-rimmed valley. A brief leftward detour at a junction brings you to the Petroglyphs. In less-enlightened times, the native rock art was painted over by a film crew in order to make it more visible to the camera's eye.

Back on the main trail, you'll parallel some cliffs, perhaps get a glimpse of some Indian bedrock mortars, and loop back to the parking area.

Contemplate the ever-changing reflections of the Wonderland Rocks on the water.

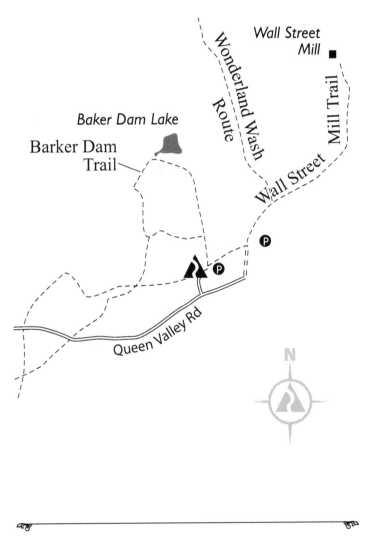

Wall Street
Mill

Wonderland Wash Route

Mill Trail

Baker Dam Lake

Barker Dam
Trail

Wall Street

Queen Valley Rd

N

WONDERLAND WASH

WONDERLAND WASH TRAIL

To Astrodomes is 2 miles round trip

One of the most popular ways into the Wonderland of Rocks is via Wonderland Wash, used by rock climbers to gain access to the Astrodomes—steep 300-foot-high rocks. It's a use trail, flat and easy to follow.

DIRECTIONS: From Park Boulevard, 1.5 miles north of the intersection with Keys View Road, turn north on the signed road to Wonderland of Rocks and drive 1.5 miles to the large parking area

THE HIKE: Begin on Wall Street Mill Trail heading east. At the first fork, go left to the ruins of a pink adobe, the Worth Bagley House. Head into the wash and follow an intermittent trail through boulder clusters and past oak and prickly pear cactus. A mile of wash-walking leads to the Astrodomes.

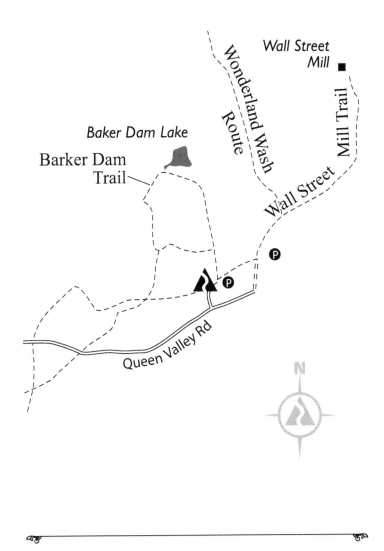

Wall Street
Mill

Wall Street Mill Trail

Wonderland Wash
Route

Baker Dam Lake

Barker Dam
Trail

Wall Street

Queen Valley Rd

N

WALL STREET MILL

WALL STREET MILL TRAIL

From Wonderland Trailhead to Wall Street Mill is 2.2 miles round trip

A mine, a mill and a murder figure prominently in the colorful history of the old mining road (now a hiking trail) on the border of the Wonderland of Rocks.

Bill Keys built the Wall Street Mill in order to process ore from his Desert Queen Mine, as well as ore from other mines scattered across the desert. The mill operated from the 1930s to 1960s, with one major interruption.

Actually, a homicidal interruption. Keys was in frequent conflict with neighbor Worth Bagley whose land was crossed by the road to Wall Street Mill. The conflict escalated, and guns were used to settle the dispute. A stone marker along the road summed up the result of the gunplay: "Here is where Worth Bagley bit the dust at the hand of W.F. Keys, May 11, 1943."

Yes, that's 1943 not 1873, and the deadly deed done in California not the Old West. In fact, by that late date, Joshua Tree has already been preserved as a national monument and was becoming an increasingly popular travel destination.

Convicted of manslaughter, Bill Keys was sent to San Quentin and served five years. Keys' contention that Bagley had threatened him and that he acted in self-defense fell on sympathetic ears. His parole from prison was due in part to the efforts of state politicians and Erle Stanley Gardner, California attorney and author of the popular Perry Mason mystery novels.

This hike visits Wall Street Mill, a fine and well-preserved example of a 1930s-1940s-era ore processing operation. Period cars and trucks are parked near the old mill.

DIRECTIONS: From Park Boulevard, 1.5 miles north of the intersection with Keys View Road, turn north on the signed road to Wonderland of Rocks and drive 1.5 miles to the large parking area. Reach a second trailhead by following Queen Valley Road briefly to meet a dirt road and driving 0.25 mile to a smaller lot.

THE HIKE: Follow the signed trail (to the right of the restrooms) along the sandy old road. Detour left to visit the pink adobe ruins of the Keys ranch house, then retrace your steps back to the main trail.

After 0.3 mile, the trail passes the second parking lot/trailhead. Look for a windmill to the right. At the 0.8-mile mark, reach an interpretive sign (sadly the original stone marker was vandalized and had to be removed) that tells of Worth Bagley's demise.

The route narrows, descends into a wash, and soon delivers you to the Wall Street Mill with its large two-stamp mill, old trucks and cyanide tanks.

Interpretation at the site includes a blueprint (circa 1931) of the mine's ambitious operation. What is so intriguing for the visitor is that so many components of the schematic are still visible on the ground: rail tracks, winch, well, pump and much more. Looks like with a few repairs, operations could start right up again!

Add the scene of a murder to this hike into history and to Wall Street Mill.

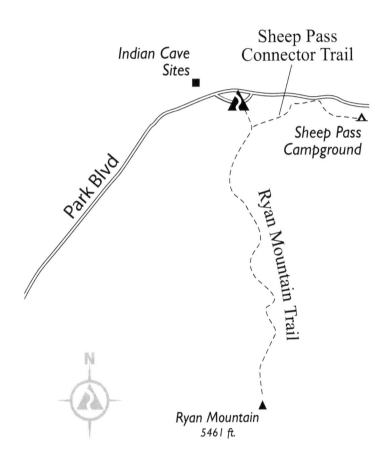

Indian Cave
Sites

Sheep Pass
Connector Trail

Sheep Pass
Campground

Park Blvd

Ryan Mountain Trail

N

Ryan Mountain
5461 ft.

Ryan Mountain

Ryan Mountain Trail

To Ryan Mountain is 3 miles round trip with 800-foot elevation gain

The path to Ryan Mountain is a superb example of the trail builder's art. Stone steps have been crafted (from the abundant supply of rocks found nearby!) and well integrated into steeper sections of the route to Ryan's roundish summit.

Ryan Mountain is named for the Ryan brothers, Thomas and Jep, who had a homestead at the base of the mountain. The views from atop Ryan Mountain, located near the center of the park, are impressive to say the least. From the 5,457-foot summit, enjoy far-reaching vistas of vast Joshua tree forests, the Wonderland of Rocks and many more of the highlights that make this national park so special.

At the west end of the trailhead parking lot, note the brief and well-worn trail leading to Indian Cave. Bedrock mortars found in the cave suggest its use as a work site by its aboriginal inhabitants. It's typical of the kind of shelter sought by the nomadic Cahuilla and Serrano Indian clans that traveled this desert land.

DIRECTIONS: From Park Boulevard, 2 miles east of its junction with Keys View Road, look for the signed turnoff for Ryan Mountain on the south side of the road. Park in the large lot.

THE HIKE: Hike south through what seems like a natural granite gateway. In 0.2 mile, reach a side trail that passes through a lunar landscape of rocks and Joshua trees and leads to Sheep Group Camp (also an alternate trailhead for this hike).

Continuing past the junction, Ryan Mountain Trail ascends moderately-to-steeply toward the peak. En route, pass very old rocks, which make up the core off this mountain and the nearby Little San Bernardino range. For eons, these rocks have, since their creation, been metamorphosed by heat and pressure into completely new types, primarily gneiss and schist.

You don't have to reach the top to get good views. Look out from the west slope of the mountain at the Little San Bernardino Mountains off to the west. A half-mile out, it's the granite formations on the face of Ryan Mountain that capture the hiker's attention.

The path works its way up to the ridgeline at the 1-mile mark. While we hikers appreciate JT's hikes up washes and along old mining roads, it's great to take a hike on well-designed and built trail like the one on Ryan Mountain.

Look out at Ryan Mountain's false summits to the north and east as you ascend the last 0.5 mile (with a stiff 400-foot elevation gain) to the true summit, marked by a pile of rocks.

The view from atop Ryan Mountain is one of the finest in the park. Right down below to the west is Ryan Campground and Ryan Ranch. Take in panoramic views of Lost Horse, Queen, Hidden and Pleasant valleys as well as clear-day vistas of the San Jacinto Mountains and San Bernardino Mountains, including SoCal high point Mount San Gorgonio.

Right from the start, there's no doubt where Ryan Mountain Trail goes.

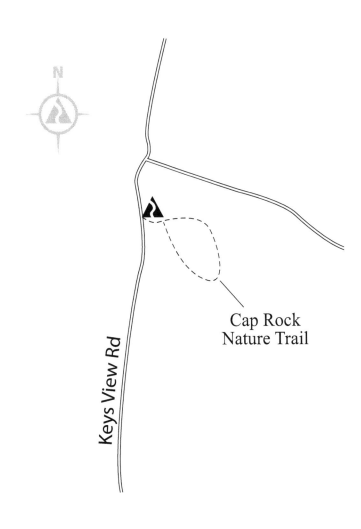

Cap Rock
Nature Trail

Keys View Rd

Cap Rock

Cap Rock Nature Trail

0.4 mile loop

Perched atop a monolithic dome is a visor-shaped boulder resembling the bill on a baseball cap. Signs along the wheelchair-accessible nature trail interpret Mojave Desert geology and plant life.

Cap Rock was a favorite spot of country-rock legend Gram Parsons. Fans maintain a modest memorial to the musician at the rock.

DIRECTIONS: From the park's west entrance, follow Park Blvd 15 more miles south to a junction and turn right on Keys View Road. The signed parking area for Cap Rock is located just 0.1 mile down the road from the intersection on the left (east) side of Keys View Road.

THE HIKE: The path loops among boulder formations and affords good views of Cap Rock and the many climbers who scale it.

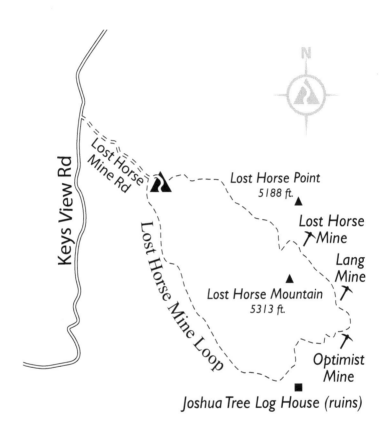

Keys View Rd

Lost Horse Mine Rd

Lost Horse Mine Loop

Lost Horse Point
5188 ft.

Lost Horse Mine

Lang Mine

Lost Horse Mountain
5313 ft.

Optimist Mine

Joshua Tree Log House (ruins)

LOST HORSE MINE

LOST HORSE MINE TRAIL

To Lost Horse Mine is 4 miles round trip with 400-foot elevation gain; loop is 6.2 miles

Lost Horse Mine was the most successful gold mining operation in this part of the Mojave. More than 9,000 ounces of gold were processed from ore dug here in the late 1890s. The mine's 10-stamp mill still stands, along with a couple of large cyanide settling tanks and a huge winch used on the main shaft. The trail to the mine offers a close-up look back into a colorful era and some fine views into the heart of the national park.

Many are the legends that swirl like the desert winds around the Lost Horse Mine. As the story goes, Johnny Lang in 1893 was camping in Pleasant Valley when his horse got loose. He tracked it out to the ranch belonging to Jim McHaney, who told Lang his horse was "no longer lost" and threatened Lang's health and future.

Lang wandered over to the camp of fellow prospector Dutch Diebold, who told him that he, too, had been threatened by McHaney and his cowboys. A pity too, because he, Diebold had discovered a promising gold prospect, but had been unable to mark his claim's boundaries. After sneaking in to inspect the claim, Johnny Lang and his father, George, purchased all rights from Diebold for $1,000.

At first it looked like a bad investment, because the Langs were prevented by McHaney's thugs from reaching their claim. Partners came and went, and by 1895, Johnny Lang owned the mine with the Ryan brothers, Thomas and Jep.

Peak production years for the mine were 1896 through 1899. Gold ingots were hidden in a freight wagon and transported to Indio. The ruse fooled any would-be highwaymen.

But thievery of another sort plagued the Lost Horse Mine. The theft was of amalgam, lumps of quicksilver from which gold could later be separated. Seems in this matter of amalgam, the mill's day shift, supervised by Jep Ryan, far out-produced the night shift, supervised by Lang. One of Ryan's men espied Lang stealing part of the amalgam. When Ryan gave Lang a choice—sell his share of the mine for $12,000 or go to the penitentiary—Lang sold out.

DIRECTIONS: From Park Boulevard, 2.5 miles south of Keys View Road, turn left on signed dirt road for Lost Horse Mine and travel 1 mile southeast to road's end, parking, and the signed trailhead.

THE HIKE: The trail, the old mine road, climbs above the left side of a wash. Pinyon pine and the nolina (often mistaken for a yucca) dot the wash. Nolina leaves are more flexible than those of yucca, and its flowers smaller.

A bit short of 2 miles, Lost Horse Mine comes into view. Note the stone foundations opposite the mill site. A little village for mine workers was built here in the late 1890s. Scramble up to the top of the hill (Lost Horse Point, elevation 5,188 feet) above the mine for a panoramic view of Queen Valley, Pleasant Valley and the desert beyond. Return the same way or complete the loop (4.2 miles).

Lost Horse Mine, once the most successful gold mining operation in this part of the Mojave.

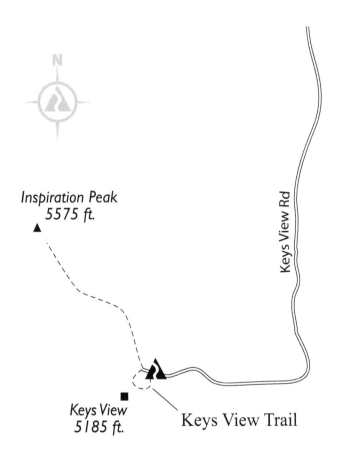

Inspiration Peak
5575 ft.

Keys View Rd

Keys View Trail

Keys View
5185 ft.

KEYS VIEW

INSPIRATION PEAK TRAIL

From Keys View to Inspiration Peak is 1.5 miles round trip with 400-foot elevation gain

Hikers know that the very best views aren't always found by following short paved trails to official, guardrail-lined park overlooks. Keys View is a case in point. This viewpoint, arguably the best in the national park, offers magnificent vistas by any standard; however, the vistas are even better from adjacent Inspiration Peak.

A wheelchair-accessible path leads to the Keys View, named for Bill Keys, rancher, miner and Joshua Tree's most colorful character. A footpath ascends to Inspiration Peak.

At 5,558 feet in elevation, Inspiration Peak is a bit higher than such well-known park summits as Warren Peak, Eureka Peak and Ryan Mountain and the view offered unequaled. A short but steep climb to the peak rewards the hiker with all the vistas available from Keys Point plus additional panoramas of the national park and a glimpse of the mountains in Mexico.

Keys View and Inspiration Peak are perched on the crest of the Little San Bernardino Mountains, a rather mellow appearing range when viewed from the north side. From the crest, however, the mountains are anything but gentle appearing as the south side plunges precipitously thousands of feet toward the Coachella Valley far below.

Clear-day views encompass the Coachella Valley with the Salton Sea shimmering mirage-like at the valley's south end. The Santa Rosa and San Jacinto Mountains (crowned by 10,894-foot Mt. San Jacinto) form the valley's far wall. Mighty Mt. San Gorgonio (11,499 feet), the Southland's highest peak, is visible to the northwest.

It's often quite breezy atop Keys View and Inspiration Peak and on days when smog obscures Palm Springs and its desert suburbs, I'm overtaken with the urge to send some fresh air down below where it's so obviously needed. Park service interpretive displays explain the effects of air pollution on the valley, the park and the Keys View view.

Another exhibit highlights the San Andreas Fault. From the southwest side of the ridge the fault is visible far below as it extends across the Coachella Valley. It's an impressive view of the famed 700-mile long fault that cuts through California to the coast north of San Francisco.

DIRECTIONS: From Highway 62 in Joshua Tree (the town), head south on Park Boulevard 15 miles to Cap Rock Junction at the turnoff for Keys View. Continue south 6 miles to road's end and parking.

THE HIKE: First join the paved, all-access path to Keys View and partake of the fine vistas. Retrace your steps and locate the beginning of unsigned Inspiration Peak Trail, on the north side of the parking lot.

As you ascend steeply above Keys View, ever more expansive vistas unfold. Continue past Inspiration Peak's first summit to a second higher one, crowned by piles of dark boulders.

Keys View, best in JT, may also be the most popular place for a selfie.

In the eye of the beholder: Skull Rock.

EVERY TRAIL TELLS A STORY.

IV

QUEEN VALLEY

HIKE ON.

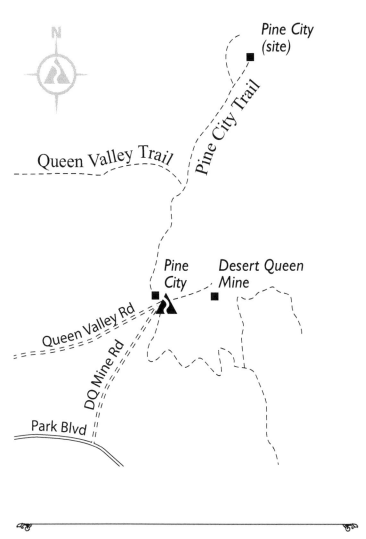

Pine City
(site)

N

Pine City Trail

Queen Valley Trail

Pine
City

Desert Queen
Mine

Queen Valley Rd

DQ Mine Rd

Park Blvd

Desert Queen Mine

Desert Queen Mine Trail

1.6 miles round trip

Perched atop cliffs north of Jumbo Rocks Campground are the considerable ruins of the Desert Queen Mine, one of the more profitable gold mines dug in the desert we now call Joshua Tree National Park. Shafts, stone building foundations, and rusting machinery are scattered about the slopes above Desert Queen Wash.

If murder and intrigue are what fascinate us about desert mines, then the Desert Queen is quite a story. The tale begins in 1894 when a prospector named Frank James discovered some rich gold ore in the hills north of Jumbo Rocks. Word of his discovery reached cattle rustler Jim McHaney who, as the story goes, ordered his men to follow James to his claim and talk things over.

One of McHaney's thugs, Charles Martin shot James dead (though an inquest jury decided Martin acted in self-defense and did not need to stand trial). Jim McHaney and his more respectable brother Bill owned the Desert Queen for two years; however, the $30,000 to $40,000 yielded from a good-sized pocket of ore was squandered by high-living Jim (who was later convicted of counterfitting) and the bank reclaimed the mine.

Hard-rock miner William Keys took control of the mine in 1915, Altadena jeweler Frederick Morton in 1931. Morton was convinced by a dubious "mining engineer" to acquire and to invest heavily in the Desert Queen. Against all odds, the miners under the supervision of "Mr. Hapwell" actually struck pay dirt. Hapwell sent diggings to a secret stamp mill nearby to process the ore and, of course, pocketed the profits. Meanwhile the fast-going-broke Morton sold stock in the Desert Queen without incorporating—a violation of securities law that soon got him convicted of fraud. The mysterious (and by some accounts wealthy) Mr. Hapwell, dropped out of sight.

On this hike you'll glimpse the Desert Queen site from an overlook and then continue down to the operation's ruins. The huge amount of ore tailings testify to the longevity (1895-1961) as well as to the considerable success of the gold mine.

DIRECTIONS: From its intersection with Pinto Basin Road, drive 5 miles west on Park Boulevard to Desert Queen Mine Road (opposite signed Geology

Tour Road). Turn right (north) on Desert Queen Mine Road and drive 1.4 miles to road's end and parking for the hikes to Desert Queen Mine and Pine City.

THE HIKE: The path, an old mine road, heads east and soon passes the stone foundation ruins of a cabin, complete with bed frame inside. After 0.25 mile, reach an overlook and regard what's left of one of this desert's most productive gold mines.

The trail descends past an information panel into the wash. Hike up the canyon bottom to view the ruins, including many fenced-off shafts. Most prominent are the piles of ore tailings and two cyanide tanks.

No city, but pinyon pine aplenty at Pine City.

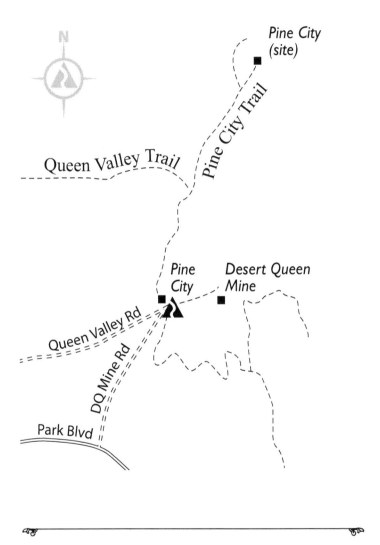

Pine City
(site)

Pine City Trail

Queen Valley Trail

Pine City

Desert Queen Mine

Queen Valley Rd

DQ Mine Rd

Park Blvd

PINE CITY

PINE CITY TRAIL

To Pine City is 3.4 miles round trip with 100-foot elevation gain

The name Pine City is a half-truth. It's not a city, just a long-abandoned mining camp. But pines it has: this bold, boulder-piled country is prime habitat for pinyon pine. Turbinella oak and juniper join the pines and weave dark green designs onto the desert tapestry.

DIRECTIONS: From Park Boulevard, head north on dirt Desert Queen Mine Road and drive 1.4 miles to road's end.

THE HIKE: March along the old mining road across Joshua tree-dotted terrain. Your route crosses several washes. About a mile out, approach great jumbles of boulders. Stands of pinyon pine herald your arrival at Pine City. Explore the many unusual rock formations and a couple of fenced mine shafts.

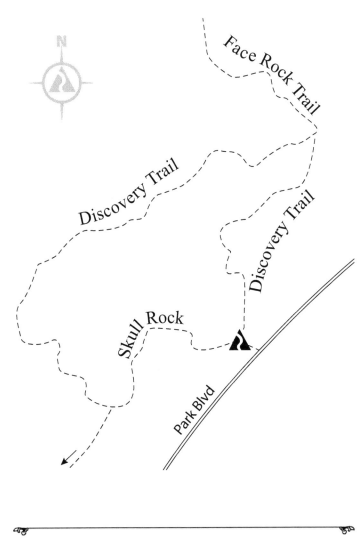

Face Rock Trail

Discovery Trail

Discovery Trail

Skull Rock

Park Blvd

SKULL ROCK

DISCOVERY, SKULL ROCK TRAILS

0.7 mile-loop

Discovery Trail, created by students from Morongo Unified School District in cooperation with park rangers, highlights 10 natural features that kids of all ages are sure to enjoy. Highlights include a slot canyon and intriguing Face Rock.

Famed and well-named Skull Rock is one of the many rocks in the area that appear to resemble humans, monsters, cathedrals and castles.

DIRECTIONS: The hike begins from the Skull Rock parking area off Park Boulevard, 3 miles west of Pinto Basin Road and just east of Jumbo Rocks Campground.

THE HIKE: Beginning as Face Rock Trail, Discovery Trail loops around to reconnect with Skull Rock Trail (a 1.7 mile loop). Half this hike is a nature trail amidst the pint-sized turbinella oak and teddy bear cholla; the other half winds among the towering rock monoliths.

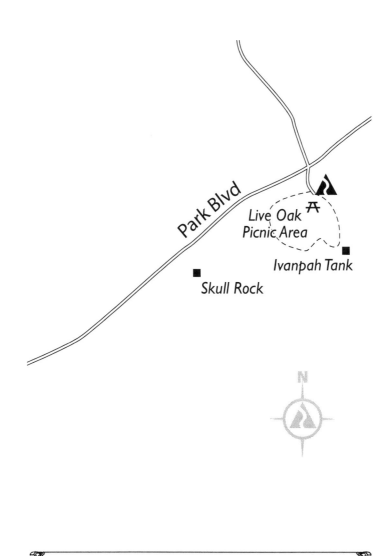

Park Blvd

Live Oak
Picnic Area

Ivanpah Tank

Skull Rock

N

IVANPAH TANK

TANK TRAIL

To Live Oak and Ivanpah Tanks is 1-mile loop

This hike travels a handsome little desert wash to visit Ivanpah Tank and Live Oak Tank, two of the many tanks built by early 20th-century cattle ranchers.

DIRECTIONS: The unsigned path begins at the end of Live Oak Picnic Area road.

THE HIKE: From the picnic area, head south toward the big old oak located at the base of the rock cluster known as the Pope's Hat. Down-canyon a short distance from the "Live Oak" is a low stone wall—what remains of Live Oak Tank.

The sandy wash angles east below rocky, juiper-dotted canyon walls, soon opens up a bit and reaches sand-filled Ivanpah Tank. Ascend the left wall of the wash and return to the picnic ground by a dirt road.

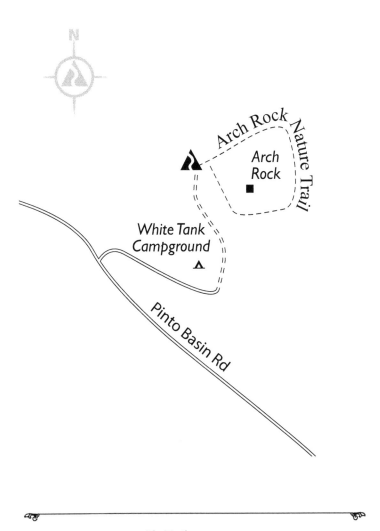

ARCH ROCK

ARCH ROCK NATURE TRAIL

0.5 mile loop

The natural arch, 135 million years in the making, looks like it might be a scaled-down version of the great sandstone arches of the American Southwest, but actually is a special variety of igneous rock known as White Tank granite.

The area's unique geology is detailed by trailside signs and displays.

DIRECTIONS: From a junction with Park Boulevard, drive 3 miles south on Pinto Basin Road to the turnoff (left) for White Tank Campground.

THE HIKE: The trail curves through intriguing stone formations to the base of the arch. Arch Rock extends some 15 feet skyward and spans about 30 feet. Before joining the return leg of the loop, visit White Tank, the old cattle tank that gave a variety of granite its name.

Roadside reminder:
Take a hike in Cholla Cactus Garden.

EVERY TRAIL TELLS A STORY.

V
PINTO BASIN &
COTTONWOOD SPRING

HIKE ON.

Pinto Basin Rd

Cholla Cactus Garden
Nature Trail

N

CHOLLA CACTUS GARDEN

CHOLLA CACTUS GARDEN NATURE TRAIL

0.25-mile loop

Highlight of this easy path is a dense concentration of Bigelow cholla, often called "teddy bear" cactus because of the (deceptively) soft, even fluffy appearance of its sharp spines. A closer look reveals a cholla that's not really fuzzy-wuzzy like a teddy bear, but more like the acupuncturist from hell armed with thousands of fine needles.

DIRECTIONS: From its junction with Park Boulevard, follow Pinto Basin Road 12 miles to Cholla Cactus Garden on the south side of the road.

THE HIKE: The beauty of this path is in the abundant Bigelows and views out to the Pinto Mountains to the north and the Hexie Mountains to the southwest.

Pinto Mountain
3983 ft.

Sand Dunes

Route to Sand Dunes

Turkey Flats

Pinto Basin Rd

N

Pinto Basin Dunes

Pinto Basin Trail

From Turkey Flats to sand dunes is 2 miles round trip

As a habitat for humans, Pinto Basin is, to say the least, forbidding: a barren lowland surrounded by austere mountains, and punctuated by sand dunes.

Nevertheless, some 4,000 to 8,000 years ago, native people lived here. Environmental conditions were friendlier then—creeks flowed across the center of the basin and a forest cloaked the mountainsides.

Still, even in these better times, the people who lived here had to make adaptations to desert living and forge some specialized tools; so unique were these ancients, anthropologists describe them as "Pinto Man." Gifted amateur archeologists from Twentynine Palms, William and Elizabeth Campbell began recovering artifacts from the Pinto Basin in the 1930s. Since then, evidence of "Pinto Man Culture" has been found in other widely scattered parts of the California Desert.

While today's visitor has a difficult time imagining how even the most primitive of people could have survived in the harsh environs of the Pinto Basin, real estate developers of the 1920s were not at all discouraged by the forbidding land and began selling parcels for homes and ranches. The Lake County Development Syndicate promised would-be buyers that an investment in Pinto Basin real estate would soon pay off big time—as soon a water source was developed. The water never came of course, and the Depression of the 1930s ended the developer's scheme.

A large, fairly-flat valley with large mountain ranges around it, the basin is quite different terrain than elsewhere in the western part of the national park. Geologists say this land is on the edge of the Basin and Range province and shares many of the characteristics of the dry lands of Nevada, Utah and eastern Oregon.

The fine soil of Pinto Basin retains sufficient moisture to support desert scrub communities and offer habitat for desert tortoises and jackrabbits. (Watch your footing; tortoise burrows dot the desert floor.)

Don't be disappointed to learn the sand dunes aren't, technically speaking, true dunes, but layers of fine sand spread over an elevated ridge along a fracture in the valley floor.

The hike to Pinto Basin's sand dunes begins at Turkey Flats, site of an unsuccessful poultry farm in the 1920s. In spring, the vast flatlands are bedecked with wildflowers, including lilies, lupine, and desert primrose. No maintained trail leads to the dunes; instead you hike N-NE toward the ridgeline visible from the trailhead.

DIRECTIONS: The Turkey Flats Backcountry Board and parking area is just off Pinto Basin Road, about 16 miles south of the Pinto Y junction and 14 miles north of Cottonwood Spring Visitor Center.

THE HIKE: Hike northeast toward the dunes. Keep oriented by heading straight toward prominent Pinto Mountain (3,983 feet). Be sure to look behind you as well to fix the landscape in your mind; the trailhead is hard to see on the way back.

Reach the first ridge of the dunes in about a mile. Continue to a second ridge or frolic in the sand before returning the way you came.

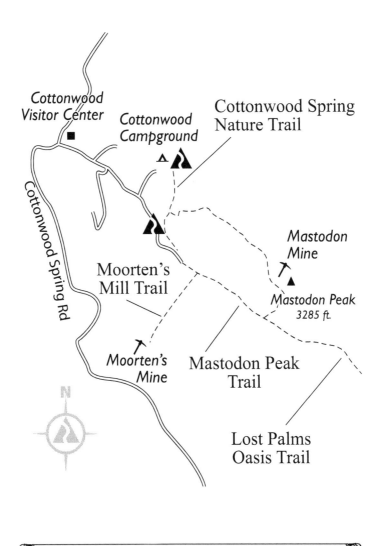

Cottonwood Visitor Center

Cottonwood Campground

Cottonwood Spring Nature Trail

Cottonwood Spring Rd

Mastodon Mine

Moorten's Mill Trail

Mastodon Peak 3285 ft.

Moorten's Mine

Mastodon Peak Trail

Lost Palms Oasis Trail

N

Cottonwood Spring Oasis

Cottonwood Spring Nature Trail

1 mile round trip

An interpreted nature trail travels through rolling hills on its way to Cottonwood Spring Oasis, haven for birds and desert wildlife. Nearby are Native American bedrock mortars.

Largely manmade Cottonwood Spring Oasis was a popular rest and overnight stop for freight-haulers and prospectors journeying from Banning to the Dale Goldfield east of Twentynine Palms. During the early 1900s, the spring's abundant waters were pumped up to the Iron Chief Mine in the Eagle Mountains.

The spring's output declined over the decades, dwindling to just a few gallons per day. Seismic activity related to the 1971 San Fernando Earthquake prompted an increased flow of water.

One of the park's best interpretive paths, Cottonwood Spring Nature Trail extends between

Cottonwood Spring Campground and Cottonwood Spring Oasis, and can be hiked from either direction. Those hikers adhering to the save-the-best-for-last theory will start from the camp and hike to the oasis.

Author of that 1919 classic, *California Desert Trails*, Joseph Smeaton Chase delighted in his campsite among the shady trees. "With musical rustle of cottonwoods I was wafted to luxurious sleep," he wrote. And Chase added: "Cottonwood Springs is one of the few desert watering-places at which the traveler would wish to stay longer than necessity requires."

Cottonwood Visitor Center (open all year 8 a.m. to 4 p.m.) is a great first stop for travelers entering JTNP from the south. Staff at the small center are very helpful about suggesting routes of travel and hikes to take. Check out the natural history exhibits and selection of maps and guides. Water, restrooms and a picnic area are nearby.

DIRECTIONS: From Highway 62 in Twentynine Palms, travel 9 miles south on Utah Trail to the Pinto Y junction, bear left, and travel 32 miles to Cottonwood Visitor Center. Turn left and drive 1.2 miles to the Cottonwood Spring parking lot and trailhead.

From Interstate 10, some 25 miles east of Indio, exit on Cottonwood Canyon Road and head north 8 miles to Cottonwood Spring Visitor Center. Turn right and drive 1.2 miles to the Cottonwood Spring parking lot and trailhead.

You can also hike from Cottonwood Springs Campground. The trailhead is located at the eastern ends of camp loops A and B; however you may not park in a campsite.

THE HIKE: Signs en route interpret plants and animals of the Colorado Desert, which predominates in the southeastern portion of the national park. The trail explores a low desert environment of green-trunked palo verde, ironwood and cottonwood trees, spindly ocotillo plants and cholla cactus. Particularly intriguing are explanations of how the native Cahuilla used a wide variety of plants for food and medicine.

Hike highlight, coming or going, is Cottonwood Spring, where the cottonwoods and palms planted long ago by miners and desert travelers now shade a lovely oasis.

Meander Cottonwood Spring Oasis on one of the park's best interpretive paths.

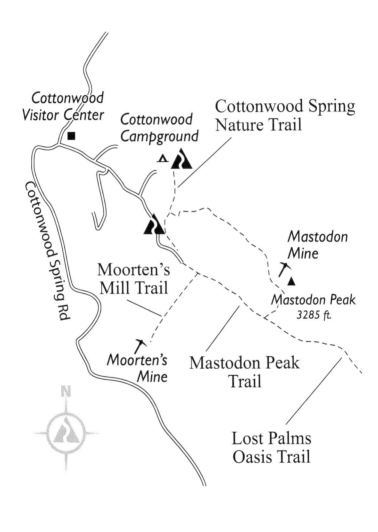

Cottonwood
Visitor Center

Cottonwood
Campground

Cottonwood Spring
Nature Trail

Cottonwood Spring Rd

Mastodon
Mine

Moorten's
Mill Trail

Mastodon Peak
3285 ft.

Moorten's
Mine

Mastodon Peak
Trail

N

Lost Palms
Oasis Trail

MASTODON PEAK
AND MASTODON MINE
MASTODON PEAK TRAIL

3-mile loop with 400-foot elevation gain

Mastodon Peak Trail offers a lot of sightseeing: a cottonwood-shaded oasis, a gold mine and grand desert views. Mastodon Peak, named for its behemoth-like profile, was the site of the Mastodon Mine, a gold mine worked from 1919 to 1932.

DIRECTIONS: From Cottonwood Spring walk back up the road 0.1 to join the nature trail.

THE HIKE: Hike the nature trail to a junction at 0.5 mile and take the right fork to the Winona mill site, shaded by eucalyptus planted by miners. Hike another mile to the shafts and ruins of Mastodon Mine and a junction; a short trail ascends Mastodon Peak. Two miles out, junction Lost Palms Trail and turn right to return to the trailhead.

Cottonwood
Visitor Center

Cottonwood Campground

Mastodon Peak Trail

Lost Palms Trail

Lost Palms Oasis

Lost Palms Oasis

Lost Palms Oasis Trail

From Cottonwood Springs to Lost Palms Oasis is 7.4 miles round trip with 300-foot elevation gain

With the help of significant underground springs, more than 100 California fan palms thrive at Lost Palms Oasis. A classic trail connects Cottonwood Oasis and Lost Palms Oasis and leads to the largest group of palms in Joshua Tree National Park.

The trail begins at largely man-made Cottonwood Spring Oasis, once a popular overnight stop for freight-haulers and prospectors during the mining years of 1870 to 1910. (See Cottonwood Spring Oasis hike description.)

While summertime is a brutal time for hikers to visit Lost Palms Oasis, it's a good time to spot wildlife, dependent on the waters and plants of the oasis for survival. Bighorn sheep frequent Lost Palms Oasis, which is day-use only for humans in order to protect the creatures' access to water.

Unlike other trails to palm oases that are straight shots up canyons to reach palm groves, Lost Palms Oasis Trail passes through a cactus garden, crosses a number of desert washes and travels up and down ridges. The path is well way-marked with signs and with arrows at turns, junctions and wash-crossings.

By the time you reach this hidden gem of an oasis you'll really feel like you're having an adventure. The memorable journey matches the destination—families of palms in a deep canyon whose steep igneous walls sparkle in the desert sun.

DIRECTIONS: From Highway 62 in Twentynine Palms, travel 9 miles south on Utah Trail to the Pinto Y junction, bear left, and travel 32 miles to Cottonwood Visitor Center. Turn left and drive 1.2 miles to the Cottonwood Spring parking lot and trailhead.

From Interstate 10, some 25 miles east of Indio, exit on Cottonwood Canyon Road and head north 8 miles to Cottonwood Spring Visitor Center. Turn right and drive 1.2 miles to the Cottonwood Spring parking lot and trailhead.

THE HIKE: From Cottonwood Spring, home to a wide variety of birds and a large number of bees, the trail marches over sandy hills, past heaps of huge rocks and along sandy draws and washes. A number of Park Service signs point the way at possibly confusing junctions.

Finally, about three miles from the trailhead, you rise above the washes and climb to an ocotillo-dotted ridge for grand desert vistas, including the Salton Sea. Dip into a minor canyon and then ascend to a rocky outcropping overlooking the canyon harboring Lost Palms Oasis at the 3.5-mile mark. From the overlook, descend the steep path around boulders to the palms.

Little surface water is present at Lost Palms Oasis, but enough is underground for the palms to remain healthy. Lost Palms remained relatively untouched throughout the mining years, though some of its water was pumped to settlements eight miles to the south at Chiriaco Summit. Adjacent to Lost Palms Canyon is a handsome upper canyon called Dike Springs. A challenging, rocky, use trail leads to another palm family known as the Victory Palms.

The journey to Lost Palms is as captivating as the destination.

Joseph Smeaton Chase, author of the classic "California Desert Trails," published in 1919.

JOSHUA TREE
STORIES

HIKE ON.

Minerva Hoyt and Her Campaign for JTNP

"The International Deserts League" Americana Magazine, July 1931 by Minerva Hoyt

Until comparatively recent times this country remained a thinly settled land. It seemed that the plentitude of natural resources could never be adequately exploited and that the teeming flora and fauna would never be exhausted and the scenic beauty of the country marred or destroyed. But the denudation of forest land, the partial or complete extinction of much interesting animal life, and the triumph of

Minerva Hoyt looked like she'd be more comfortable at the opera than in the great outdoors, but she was a formidable champion of the desert.

scientific irrigation over natural conditions inimical to agriculture have shown us how illusory that confidence was. When men need land for agricultural purposes they usually obtain it, as has been demonstrated in the conversion of former waste land of the Imperial Valley in California into an area rich in its many crops of fruit, vegetables and cotton.

Desert land is no more safe from exploitation than forest land has been. If we wish to preserve any portion of it for posterity and to protect its rare and beautiful flora and fauna in their natural habitat we must see to it that parks and reservations are created in which the unique desert atmosphere and its matchless growth and its silence and mystery are preserved for the education and delight of the people.

Minerva Hoyt was known as "Apostle of the Cacti" for her crusade on behalf of desert protection.

The Joshua Tree

U-2's The Joshua Tree is often listed as one of the greatest rock albums of all time. Hit songs from the album, released in 1987, include "I Still Haven't Found What I'm Looking For," "Where the Streets Have No Name" and "With Or Without You."

U-2's The Joshua Tree, one of the all-time great rock albums.

The album's enduring popularity keeps it at the top of the Google Search for "Joshua Tree," even above Joshua Tree National Park, ranked second in search engines.

As the story goes, Bono was fascinated by the tale of the tree's name (it reminded early settlers of the prophet Joshua, its limbs resembling arms raised to the heavens in prayer). He thought the Joshua tree captured the spiritually conscious feel of the band's music. The now iconic album cover features the Irish rockers posed in the Mojave Desert and a Joshua Tree graces the back cover.

"U-2's Joshua Tree," located in Joshua Tree National Park, has become a memorial and pilgrimage site for fans from around the world.

"Introductory" from *California Desert Trails* (published in 1919) by Joseph Smeaton Chase.

Chase left us a lyrical account of two years of desert adventures, including exploration of what is now Joshua Tree National Park.

The desert is the opposite of all that we naturally find pleasing. Yet I believe that its hold upon those who have fallen under its spell is deeper and more enduring than is the charm of forest or sea or mountain. This must seem a strange statement to make, but I make it with consideration and in the light of others experience besides my own. The beauty of the great woodlands, the mystical solemnity of the sea, the power and glory of mountains—right well we love all these: yet somehow, that pale, grave face of the desert, if once you look upon it, take you more subtly captive and keeps you enchained by a stronger bond.

It is as if you were bemused by the grace of a sorceress: or had listened over long to some witching, monotonous strain: or had pondered too deeply on old legends of weirdry or parchments from tombs of strange, forgotten lands. Certainly it is not love, in any degree, that one feels for the desert, nor could any other single term convey the sentiment. But whatever it is, there is something haunting in it, and it is a haunting that lasts a lifetime.

After centuries of home, security, satisfaction of want, we come to a revulsion. Ease and tame ways of living have reached, for most of us, the present far stage, there has arisen a zest for things rugged and wild. Hardship looks attractive, scarcity becomes desirable, starkness turns an unexpected side of beauty.

As scenery merely, the desert is the last field one could take the fancy. The forest, even if gloomy, gives a sense of companionship, and is filled with life and the means of life—food, fire, and shelter. The mountains give pleasant boundary to our little lives, shutting out strange humanity and alien climes, and vaguely gratifying the sentiment for home. But the desert yields no point of sympathy, and meets every need of man with a cold, repelling No.

The metaphysical must be reckoned with after all to explain the strange attraction of the desert. Space, solitude and quiet—our minds at their best are tuned to these, and when they find them they expand like the anemone welcoming its native tide.

Is there attraction in this, then? To most people, No. To a few, Yes, and Yes to an increasing number, I think and hope, as the loud roar grows louder; the times more complex and out of joint; the strife of tongues more clever and useless; simplicity, the touchtone of good, less than ever revered.

The Man From the Cave

The great hiker and author (*The Man Who Walked Through Time, The Complete Backpacker*) Colin Fletcher discovered a lonely cave with evidence that a remarkable man lived there in the early 20th century. *Man From the Cave*, published in 1981, is a kind of detective story of Fletcher over the course of a dozen years, uncovering the identity of soldier and prospector Anthony William Simmons, aka Chuckawalla Bill. Coincidentally, Simmons turns out to be a wanderer, just like Fletcher.

In an obscure wash in a wilderness area of Joshua Tree National Park, the author found a cabin where Bill lived from 1932 to about 1936. *The Man from the Cave* is a good read, and full of the kind of trailside philosophizing that makes Fletcher such a special author.

Colin Fletcher inspired a generation of hikers with his books "The Man Who Walked Through Time" and "The Complete Backpacker."

"Mostly, two miles an hour is good going," Fletcher wrote. Words to live by for hikers, for everyone—especially now in our hurry-up world.

From a cave in Nevada to a cabin in Joshua Tree National Park, Colin Fletcher traces the life of the curious Bill Simmons.

Death Valley NP
Yosemite National Park
Lava Beds NM
Joshua Tree National Park
Pinnacles NP
Eugene O'Neill NHS
Muir Woods NM
Whiskeytown-Shasta Trinity NRA
Golden Gate National Recreation Area
Devils Postpile NM
Lassen Volcanic National Park
Cabrillo NM
Channel Islands National Park
Redwood NP
Mojave NPRES
César Chávez NM
John Muir NHS
Rosie the Riveter NHS
Santa Monica Mountains NRA
Point Reyes NS
Sequoia-Kings Canyon National Parks

CALIFORNIA'S NATIONAL PARKS

Other states have national parks with tall trees, high peaks, deep canyons, long seashores and vast deserts, but only California can claim all these grand landscapes within its boundaries.

California boasts nine national parks, the most in the nation. In addition, the state's national parklands include national recreation areas, national monuments, national historic parks, a national seashore and a national preserve.

The state features one of America's oldest national parks—Yosemite set aside in 1890—and one of its newest—César E. Chávez National Monument established in 2012.

Mere acreage does not a national park make, but California's national parks include the largest park in the contiguous U.S.—3.3-million acre Death Valley National Park. Yosemite (748,542 acres) and Joshua Tree (790,636 acres) are also huge by any park standards. Even such smaller parklands as Redwoods National Park and Pt. Reyes National Seashore are by no means small.

California and The National Park Idea

Not long after John Muir walked through Mariposa Grove and into the Yosemite Valley, California's natural treasures attracted attention worldwide and conservationists rallied to preserve them as parks. As the great naturalist put it in 1898: "Thousands of nerve-shaken, overcivilized people are beginning to find out that going to the mountains is going home; that wilderness is a necessity; and that mountain parks and reservations are useful not only as fountains of timber and irrigating rivers, but as fountains of life."

The National Park Service, founded in 1916, was initially guided by borax tycoon-turned-park-champion Stephen T. Mather and his young assistant, California attorney Horace Albright. The park service's mission was the preservation of "the scenery and the natural and historic objects and the wild life" and the provision "for the enjoyment of the same in such manner and by such means as will leave them unimpaired for the enjoyment of future generations."

The invention of the automobile revolutionized national park visitation, particularly in car-conscious California. John Muir called them "blunt-nosed mechanical beetles," yet as one California senator pointed out, "If Jesus Christ had an automobile he wouldn't have ridden a jackass into Jerusalem."

With cars came trailers, and with trailer camps came concessionaires. National parks filled with mobile cities of canvas and aluminum, and by visitors anxious to see California's natural wonders. During the 1920s and 30s, the park service constructed signs identifying scenic features and rangers assumed the role of interpreting nature for visitors.

By 1930 California had four national parks: Yosemite, Lassen, Sequoia and General Grant (Kings Canyon.) In the 1930s, two big desert areas—Joshua Tree and Death Valley—became national monuments.

With the 1960s came hotly contested, and eventually successful campaigns to create Redwood National

Steven Mather (R) and his assistant Horace Albright guided the National Park Service in its early days.

Park and Point Reyes National Seashore. During the 1970s the National Park Service established parks near the state's big cities—Golden Gate National Recreation Area on the San Francisco waterfront and Marin headlands and Santa Monica Mountains National Recreation Area, a Mediterranean ecosystem near Los Angeles. Also during that decade, Mineral King Valley was saved from a mega-ski resort development and added to Sequoia National Park. Channel Islands National Park, an archipelago offshore from Santa Barbara, was established in 1980.

During the 1980s and 1990s, major conservation battles raged in the desert. After more than two decades of wrangling, Joshua Tree and Death Valley national monuments were greatly expanded and given national park status, and the 1.6-million acre Mojave National Preserve was established under provisions of the 1994 California Desert Conservation Act.

Today, the National Park Service must address challenging questions: How best to regulate concessionaires? Should motor vehicles be banned from Yosemite Valley? How can aging park facilities cope with many years of deferred maintenance?

And the biggest issue of all: How will our parks (indeed our planet!) cope with the rapidly increasing effects of climate change?

The consequences of climate change to California's national parks is ever more apparent. In recent years, after prolonged droughts, devastating wildfires burned the Yosemite backcountry, parts of Sequoia National Park and more than half the Santa Monica Mountains National Recreation Area. Scientists have discovered that trees in Sequoia and Kings Canyon national parks endure the worst ozone levels of all national parks, in part because of their proximity to farm-belt air in the San Joaquin Valley.

California's national parklands struggle with an ever-increasing numbers of visitors. The California Office of Tourism charts visitation to national parks along with airports, hotel occupancy and other attractions such as Disneyland and Universal Studios. Yosemite is California's most-visited park with 4.5 to 5 million visitors a year, and many other parks count millions of visitors or "visitor days," per year.

What may be the saving grace of national parks is the deep-seated, multi-generational pride Americans have for their national parklands. We not only love national parks, we love the very idea of national parks. Even in an era of public mistrust toward government, national parks remain one of the most beloved institutions of American life.

National Parks have often been celebrated as America's best idea. As writer Wallace Stegner put it: "National parks are the best idea we ever had. Absolutely American, absolutely democratic, they reflect us at our best rather than our worst."

The Trails

The state of the state's national park trail system is excellent. Trailhead parking, interpretive panels and displays, as well as signage, is generally tops in the field. Backcountry junctions are usually signed and trail conditions, with a few exceptions of course, range from good to excellent.

Trail systems evolved on a park-by-park basis and it's difficult to speak in generalities about their respective origins. A good deal of Yosemite's trail system was in place before the early horseless carriages chugged into the park.

Several national parks were aided greatly by the Depression-era Civilian Conservation Corps of the 1930s. Sequoia and Pinnacles national parks, for example, have hand-built trails by the CCC that are true gems, highlighted by stonework and bridges that would no doubt be prohibitively expensive to construct today.

Scout troops, the hard-working young men and women of the California Conservation Corps and many volunteer groups are among the organizations that help park staff build and maintain trails.

The trail system in California's national parklands shares many characteristics in common with pathways overseen by other governmental bodies, and have unique qualities as well. One major difference between national parks and, for example, California's state parks, is the amount of land preserved as wilderness. A majority of Yosemite, Sequoia, Death Valley, Joshua Tree and several more parks are official federally designated wilderness. Wilderness comprises some 94 percent of Yosemite National Park, 93 percent of Death Valley National Park, and more than 80 percent of Joshua Tree National Park.

On national park maps you'll find wilderness areas delineated as simply "Wilderness." Unlike the Forest Service, the Bureau of Land Management or other wilderness stewards, the National Park Service does not name its wilderness areas.

Author John McKinney admires the sign for Yosemite's Four Mile Trail.

"Wilderness" is more than a name for a wild area. By law, a wilderness is restricted to non-motorized entry—that is to say, equestrian and foot travel. Happily, hikers do not have to share the trails with snowmobiles or mountain bikes in national park wilderness.

Because national park trails attract visitors from all over the globe, the park service makes use of international symbols on its signage, and the metric system as well. Don't be surprised if you spot trail signs with distance expressed in kilometers as well as miles and elevation noted in meters as well as feet.

The hikers you meet on a national park trail may be different from the company you keep on trails near home. California's national parks attract increasing numbers of ethnically and culturally diverse hikers of all ages, shapes and sizes, from across the nation and around the world. Once I counted ten languages on a popular trail in Yosemite! The hiking experience is much enriched by sharing the trail with hikers from literally all walks of life.

CALIFORNIA'S NATIONAL PARKLANDS

Alcatraz Island
Cabrillo National Monument
Castle Mountains National Monument
César E. Chávez National Monument
Channel Islands National Park
Death Valley National Park
Devils Postpile National Monument
Eugene O'Neill National Historic Site
Fort Point National Historic Site
Golden Gate National Recreation Area
John Muir National Historic Site
Joshua Tree National Park
Lassen Volcanic National Park
Lava Beds National Monument
Manzanar National Historic Site
Mojave National Preserve
Muir Woods National Monument
Pinnacles National Park
Point Reyes National Seashore
Port Chicago Naval Magazine National Memorial
Presidio of San Francisco
Redwood National and State Parks
Rosie the Riveter WWII Home Front National
    Historic Park
San Francisco Maritime National Historic Park
Santa Monica Mountains National Recreation Area
Sequoia and Kings Canyon National Parks
Tule Lake National Monument
Whiskeytown National Recreation Area
Yosemite National Park

THE HIKER'S INDEX

Celebrating the Scenic, Sublime and Sensational Points of Interest in California's National Parks

State with the most National Parks

California, with 9

Largest National Park in Contiguous U.S.

Death Valley with 3.3 million acres

Third Largest National Park in Contiguous U.S.

Mojave National Preserve

Foggiest Place on the West Coast

Point Reyes Lighthouse, Point Reyes National Seashore

World's Tallest Tree

A 379.7-foot high coast redwood named Hyperion in Redwood National Park

World's Largest Tree

General Sherman Tree, 275 feet tall, with a base circumference of 102 feet, growing in the Giant Forest Area of Sequoia National Park

World's Largest-In-Diameter Tree

General Grant Tree, dubbed "the nation's Christmas tree," more than 40 feet in diameter at its base, growing in Kings Canyon National Park.

Largest Elephant Seal Population on Earth

San Miguel Island, Channel Islands National Park

Highest Point in Contiguous U.S.

Mt. Whitney (14,508 feet in elevation) on the far eastern boundary of Sequoia National Park

Lowest Point in Western Hemisphere

Badwater (282 feet below sea level) in Death Valley National Park

California's Largest Island

Santa Cruz Island, Channel Islands National Park

Only Major Metropolis Bisected by a Mountain Range

Los Angeles, by the Santa Monica Mountains (National Recreation Area)

Highest Waterfall in North America

Yosemite Falls, at 2,425 feet, in Yosemite National Park

JOHN MCKINNEY

John McKinney is an award-winning writer, public speaker, and author of 30 hiking-themed books: inspiring narratives, top-selling guides, books for children.

John is particularly passionate about sharing the stories of California trails. He is the only one to have visited—and written about—all 280 California State Parks. John tells the story of his epic hike along the entire California coast in the critically acclaimed *Hiking on the Edge: Dreams, Schemes, and 1600 Miles on the California Coastal Trail.*

For 18 years John, aka The Trailmaster, wrote a weekly hiking column for the Los Angeles Times, and has hiked and enthusiastically told the story of more than 10 thousand miles of trail across California and around the world. His "Every Trail Tells a Story" series of guides highlight the very best hikes in California.

The intrepid Eagle Scout has written more than a thousand stories and opinion pieces about hiking, parklands, and our relationship with nature.

A passionate advocate for hiking and our need to reconnect with nature, John is a frequent public speaker, and shares his tales on radio, on video, and online.

JOHN MCKINNEY:
"EVERY TRAIL TELLS A STORY."

HIKE ON.

TheTrailmaster.com

Made in the USA
Columbia, SC
13 February 2024

31436201R00088